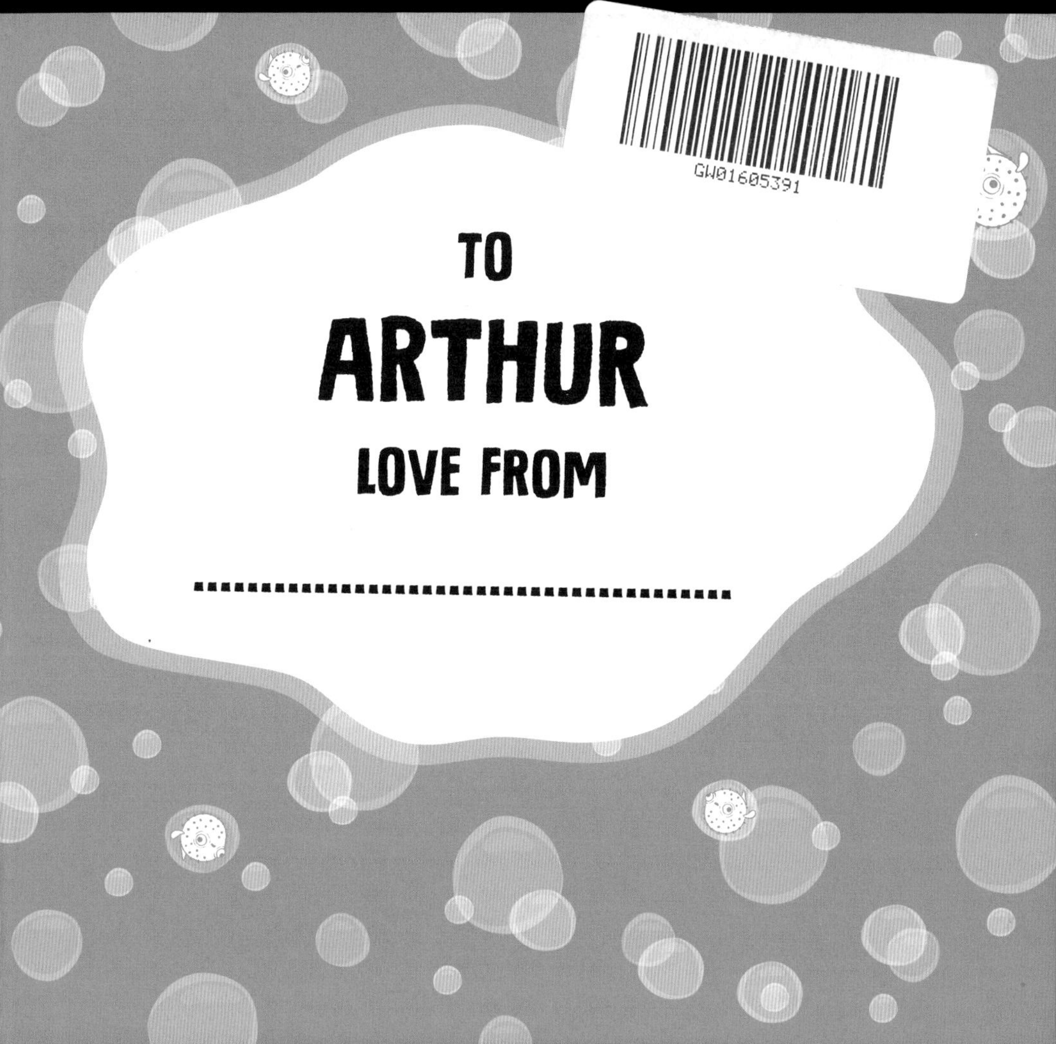
GW01605391
TO
ARTHUR
LOVE FROM

Arthur loves being under the sea. Whether it's exploring a sunken pirate ship, swimming with mighty whales or looking at big shells, he couldn't be happier.

But today was different. Arthur was about to meet the most majestic creature of the underwater world....

Arthur was gliding through the cool, clear water, hypnotised by the coral, when he heard something strange.

"Is that ... crying?" he said.

SOB! SOB! SOB!

Arthur swam towards the sound and stopped when he spotted an entrance to a deep, dark cave....

"I wonder what's in there?" Arthur thought as he drifted closer.

As he bobbed up and down a sea creature peeked out from the darkness!

"Err, he- hello?" he whispered.

Arthur could just about make out that he was pink with blue sticky-up hair. But he wasn't scary, he just looked very sad.

And he was carrying a gold crown.

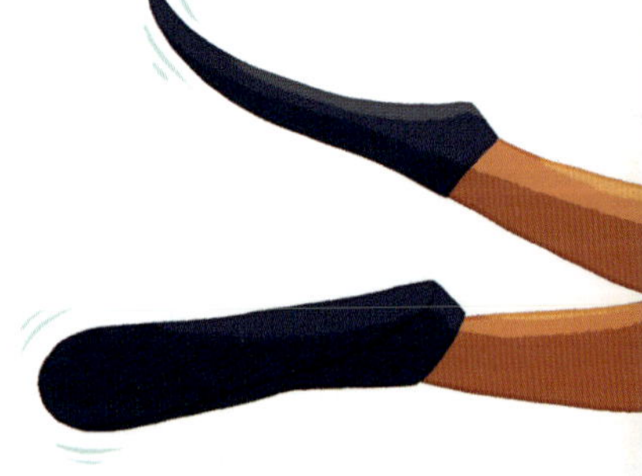

The sea creature wasn't just any old sea creature – he was a king. But he might not be for much longer.

"I was having my afternoon snooze, and when I woke up the jewels from my crown were gone," he sniffled. "If I don't get them back, how can I be king?"

"Don't worry," said Arthur. "I'll help you find them. Whoever took them can't have gone far. Let's go!"

And so the search for the lost jewels began....

"There's one!" pointed Arthur.

"Oh no, the grumpy crabs have got it!" gasped the king.

SNAP! GRUMBLE, GRUMBLE! SNAP! SNAP!

Arthur quickly dodged round one, darted past another, ducked under a third and rescued the jewel from a snapping claw.

"I've got it!" he yelled.

"Quick, let's skedaddle," said the king. "They'll be grumpier than ever now!"

Up ahead, Arthur and the king saw a giant clamshell perched on a rock. Could a jewel be trapped inside?

"Hmm," said Arthur, "how do you get a clamshell to open up?"

"I don't know," said the king, "how do you get a clamshell to open up?"

"It's not a joke!" said Arthur, "but that gives me an idea...."

He grabbed a handful of seaweed and began to tickle.

HA HA HA! HA HA HA! HA HA HA!

The clamshell burst open and the king plucked out the jewel.

"Ta-dah, only two more left to find!" he cheered.

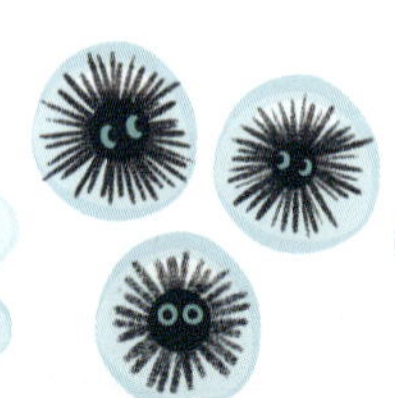

Suddenly, a dolphin whooshed past and darted upwards.

"Something fishy's going on," giggled Arthur, "let's go!"

They burst onto the surface where a pod of dolphins was jumping and spinning and diving.

SPLASH! SPLISH! SPLOSH!

And they were throwing around another jewel.

Arthur had to act fast. He threw his wallet up in the air to trick the dolphins. Then, he quickly caught the jewel.

"Three down, only one to go!" he smiled.

The only place left on the reef they hadn't searched was ...

THE SEAWEED FOREST!

"Are you s-s-sure you want to g-g-go in there?" stuttered the king nervously.

Arthur looked up at the towering hairy branches swaying back and forth. Big, spooky eyes blinked back at him from the darkness, but that didn't stop him.

"I'll be fine!" said Arthur as he flicked on his torch.

Arthur hadn't been in an underwater forest before, but it was fun.

As he swam upwards he suddenly came face-to-face with the cutest thing he'd ever seen – a gigantic octopus.

The octopus looked startled and darted off. And as he did, eagle-eyed Arthur spotted the last jewel.

"Come back!" he shouted.

But the octopus disappeared.

Arthur needed a plan.

He kicked his flippers harder and harder and swam faster and faster through the seaweed to get ahead of the octopus.

Then he stopped, hid and kept very still.

It wasn't long before the seaweed started to rustle. He waited for just the right moment, and then....

"BOOOO!" yelled Arthur.

"AHHHHHHHH!" wailed the octopus.

Arthur quickly jumped out and rescued the final jewel.

Arthur carefully pressed the jewels into the king's crown and swam up to place it on his head.

"Ready?" asked Arthur.

"Ready!" smiled the king.

As Arthur lowered the crown all the fishy friends let out a big cheer, and all around them looked like awesome fireworks.

WOO-HOO! HOORAY!

"Arthur, you're my hero!" declared the king.

"I can't thank you enough," said the king. "If there's anything I can do for you, just name it."

"Well, there is one small thing," smiled Arthur. "Can you please let the jewel thieves out? They were only playing."

"Consider it done," said the king, "I guess they've learned their lesson now."

And with that, Arthur turned, waved goodbye and began to swim home, daydreaming of his next BIG adventure....

TIME OUT

MEET SANTA?
Maybe I'll...

Arthur, look out for more **Mini Adventures** books.
Go to www.orangutanbooks.co.uk

Story by Jane Kent
Illustrated by Jo Lindley
Designed by Jane Gollner

First published by Orangutan Books in 2019
Hometown World Ltd, 1 Queen Street, Bath BA1 1HE

Visit
www.orangutanbooks.co.uk
Follow us @orangutanbooks

ISBN 978-1-78979-446-5

Printed in Italy
HTW_PO201907

MIX
Paper from responsible sources
FSC® C023419